AF584614

Everyone's a Critic
The Ultimate Cartoon Book
by the World's Greatest Cartoonists

EVERYONE'S A CRITIC

THE ULTIMATE CARTOON BOOK

by the

World's Greatest Cartoonists

Bob Eckstein, editor

PRINCETON ARCHITECTURAL PRESS · NEW YORK

Introduction

What's more fun than being judgmental? As a species, we relish this activity so much that we've created an entire society based around large groups of opinionated people offering their input on just about everything.

Take dating, for instance. If you've gone out lately, your date was likely chosen through an elaborate screening process on a dating site, perhaps Cupids for Cartoonists or Compromise, Already. Instead of sizing up just one person, you first judge hundreds in what amounts to a colossal beauty pageant for the unattached. Swiping left, swiping right, you scrutinize their attempts to look worldly, with their selfies at the foot of the Eiffel Tower or Machu Picchu.

After you hold your own private *Project Runway* in front of your mirror, critically assessing your own appearance, you use an Uber to get to your date because you don't have a car (please, don't judge). During your ride you critique the driver's small talk and driving skills. You make a mental note of every quick, jolting stop or missed turn, and at the end of the ride you give the trip a rating of one to five stars. Woe is the poor next passenger—after you leave only one star for the scary driving and strange smell in the car—who will have to deal with a very cranky driver.

Before you can get to any of that, you need to select a movie for the evening. Oh, wait—first, you'll need to choose the theater before you can even discuss the movie. TripAdvisor allows anyone one with the slightest ax to grind to be a critic of anything, even movie theaters. "The floor was sticky. No stars."

Now we can consider the movie. Thanks to Rotten Tomatoes, you have scores of reviews to sift through and process. It will have to be a cinematic experience on par with *Citizen Kane* or you (and your date) will be tweeting throughout the movie how bad it is.

Finding a late-night place for dinner should not be difficult. You spent four hours that afternoon on Yelp, and you've narrowed it down to twelve choices. Being happy at any of them is a different story. You conduct yourself in the chosen establishment as if it were you who hands out Michelin stars. Years of watching reality shows like *Top Chef* have distorted your dining reality, and basically, you are now impossible to feed. (The other day a waiter came over to my in-laws and asked, "Is ANYthing alright?")

That's to say nothing of the dinner conversation, as you compare your date's every witty comment to those of seasoned comics on their third or fourth Netflix comedy special. Everyone's a critic now.

Can you imagine if our ancestors used Trip Advisor instead of just hopping on a ship over here? "Do we really want to try that place? It's filled with our tired, our hungry, and our noisy." Our founding fathers had no time for reviews. The *Times* didn't pan the Donner Party ("Two thumbs down!"), telling pioneers there was nothing worth the price of admission out West. Paul Revere didn't ride the countryside announcing: "The risotto is runny! The risotto is runny!"

Our country is overrun with critics: us. All the *great* critics, like Siskel and Ebert, Judith Crist, Joel Siegel, and the two old men on the *The Muppet Show*, have gone to the great balcony in the sky. Perhaps the lesson there is it's better to bite one's tongue than to go around criticizing everyone. We bitch and moan our whole life, and where does it get us? I'm hoping this book can be a life-changing experience for those who up until now have been unable to roll with the punches or simply enjoy a chef's salad. I know it has been for me.

—*Bob Eckstein*

"That's the one I like the best, but everyone else seems to like the other one."

You call that a suit?
MEET THE REVIEWER
Shanahan

“My wife! My best friend! Advanced uncorrected galleys of my new book!”

BOOKS BETTER THAN THE MOVIES
MOVIES BETTER THAN THE BOOKS
BOOKS NEVER TURNED INTO MOVIES
BOOKS THAT NEVER SHOULD HAVE BEEN TURNED INTO MOVIES
BOOKS THAT NEVER EVER SHOULD BE TURNED INTO MOVIES
BOOKS THAT SHOULD NEVER EVER EVER BE TURNED INTO MOVIES

YOU MUST BE
THIS TALL—
TO HAVE
AN OPINION
Haefeli

“That’s totally derivative of real life.”

"I told him to come back when he's truly gifted."

STERO
STAFF PICKS

"Frankly, your mother and I think you did better work when you were two."

"Okay, fair enough—that's a great price for mayonnaise."

"You can execute everyone who calls you
'Ivan the Terrible'—or you can stop being so terrible."

"When you said we needed to talk, you didn't say I needed to listen."

"What's the takeaway on all this?"

S. GROSS

“Some wine with your vest?”

"You were a schlub in all of your previous lives, too."

"First off, there was a bee in the car."

"I can't decide if that was bad in a good way, good in a good way, good in a bad way, or bad in a bad way."

“I know this isn’t the suspect, ma’am, but is it art?”

“What riles me is that he got a genius grant and I didn't.”

"No more clubs unless you swear to never wear that outfit again."

HOT DOGS
GYROS
KEBABS
$2.00
ANTACID
BROMO
BICARB
$3.00
P. BYRNES.

“This is an opportunity to simplify your life—don’t blow it.”

10
1
THOMPSON

"Excuse me for interrupting, madam, but before you go on any further, allow me to make these comments: one, I have no desire for you to do my cooking; two, I neither want nor need you to pay my rent; three, I'm very sorry you cried the whole night long; and four, and perhaps most important, I think you've called the wrong Bill Bailey."

“If only the aftertaste came first.”

"Warning—viewer discretion is advised."

"Look, I brought it in to be cleaned, not critiqued."

“Do I really have to add ‘just kidding’ after everything I say?”

IT'S ALWAYS 'GOOD DOG'–
NEVER 'GREAT DOG.'
GREGORY

CRITIC
★
★★
★★★
★★★★
★★
★
LKEGCER

"If it please Your Honor, may I redo the bench?"

CRITICAL SUCCESS
B. Smaller

NOW PLAYING
THE BLURB
NOW PLAYING
THE BLURB
"YOU'LL LAUGH, YOU'LL CRY, YOU'LL GET A WARM FEELING"
L.A. GAZETTE
XCITING!
NEW YORK MOON
"WACKY, ZANY, MADCAP"
NEWARK LEDGER
"AN EXCELLENT HIGHLY STYLIZED FRENCH FARCE!"
CHICAGO BULLETIN
"DAZZLING ACCOMPLISHED PERFORMANCES"
BROOKLYN NEWS
"FLAWLESS!"
KNBX RADIO
"ASTONISHING"
"SPECTACULAR"
HOUSTON PRESS
"SIZZLING"
INQUIRER
"A SMART AND FUNNY FILM"
BOISE STAR
"AN INSTANT CLASSIC"
"TWO THUMBS UP"
John O'Brien

“The trailer didn’t live up to the teaser.”

"Do these complement my face?"

"Why can't you just be happy for me that I'm going to Paris?"

"We never would have abducted you if we had known how much you would criticize our driving."

"I thought they introduced the witch a little late."

"I see he finally got rid of that idiotic comb-over."

Lose...the...
hat...

"You live by Rotten Tomatoes, you die by Rotten Tomatoes."

"I'd like your honest, unbiased, and possibly career-ending opinion on something."

"Arthur knows everything about theater, except how to enjoy it."

“The innocence seems forced.”

A Critique of Pure Reason

PAUL NOTH

"He saves all his critical thinking for my behavior."

“The service is terribly slow, but the food is excellent.”

“Keep in mind, this dish is best served in a restaurant, cooked by anyone other than you.”

SWIM
CRITIC
LIANA
FINCK

AND THAT'S Why I'm Still Single!
Mary
TOM & MOM
bob

"There's a restaurant critic out there.
Thaw out a meal from that place they all like."

"But what I didn't sleep through, I liked."

I AM PROUD OF MY GAY SON
I AM PROUD OF MY GAY SON
I AM PROUD OF MY GAY SON
MY GAY SON NEVER CALLS
I AM PROUD OF MY GAY SON
I AM PROUD OF MY GAYSON
S. GROSS

“Your résumé is extra-ordinary, and by that I don’t mean ‘extraordinary.’”

"Enough already with the TripAdvisor reviews."

"Whaddaya mean I'm funny? Funny how? I amuse you?
I make you laugh? Funny how? How'm I funny?"

"Did you read my review on Amazon?
Four out of four people found it helpful."

"I love what you've done with him."

OH, GOD. HERE COMES THE SPEECH.

“Let me guess—first child?”

“Great! But maybe get rid of the hats.”

"His drumming's improving."

"You call this literature?"

"It would take more than your pleats to
drive us apart, but not much more."

"The jury's still out on your cheese balls."

ROME
CARAVAGGIO
HURLED
ARTICHOKES
AT WAITERS
IN THIS
RESTAURANT
NICK DOWNES

"Jake, opinions are like podcasts, everyone has one."

"It's about your new sanitation system, sire."

"Just don't be yourself."

UNCLE TOD'S REVIEWS

★★★★ BURGER BAZAAR

I've eaten here plenty of times and never gotten sick.

★★★★ GOLDEN DRAGON

Nice place. Eaten here a lot. Never gotten sick.

★★★★ THE OYSTER BARN

I go here all the time. Never had a problem.

★★★★ HILDA'S GRUB SHACK

Eaten here at least 700 times. Only sick once.

"This is your wake-up call—change or die."

"I can't remember if I didn't like his second book or his second wife."

“I’ve only got seven ‘likes’ for what I put in my shopping cart.”

"Hey, this is brilliant! Where do you get my ideas?"

"Well, if it isn't the dawn of civilization."

HECKLERS ON POETRY NIGHT

“Minimalism, folks. Nothing to see here.”

"The 'ho ho ho' thing—we get it.
By Act II I'm looking for it to have evolved."

"I love when it all comes together... not like now of course."

“This is what happens when you over-tip.”

"If it's any consolation, that was an amazing impression of the king."

"Thank you, but we're casting *The Crucible*."

"Excuse me, but it's important to get those drinks
to those who need them the most."

“He’s a comment waiting to happen.”

"Entertain me."

"Wow! You need professional help."

"Everyone's a critic."

“Somehow I thought the coffee would be better.”

SUGGESTIONS

POPCORN CRITIC

"And finally, may I ask how satisfied you were with the way I handled your interrogation today?"

"You'll be in charge of the music down here."

"Would you say the tuna salad kicks ass?"

"Mother! Father! They let me cast the first stone!"

THANK YOU FOR
NOT RUNNING FOR
PRESIDENT
WEYANT

"All right, let's do it again. This time, you're good at acting."

The Surreal McCoy
CAFE MEH

"The coffee is so-so, but the Wi-Fi is excellent."

"It's not just the same old crap—it's wider."

I MAY NOT KNOW MUCH ABOUT ART, BUT I DO KNOW WHAT'S SUITABLE FOR FRAMING
S. GROSS

"Goodbye, Kevin.
I could look the other way with the boozing and the skirt-chasing,
but I did not sign up for bicycle clothes."

"I hope that's not the tie you're going to wear tonight."

"I heard this entire symphony yesterday, while on hold."

That's good.
Stop now.
You better
stop.
You ruined
it.

“No, actually you’re very different from the women I usually date.”

“This lamp reminds me of my late husband, because I hate it.”

"Perhaps I've said too much."

"Tell me, sir. Is it good or bad?"

“Get a load of what the *Times* thinks we ought to know.”

"Your friends and family are here, Roger, because they love you and can no longer sit idly by and watch you throw your life away on yoga classes."

"The following program is rated P, for 'poop.'"

"Would you mind taking a look at this collection of my poems? Your opinion would mean a lot."

LOSE THE CAP.

"If it's not scratched in the dirt with a stick, it's not Art."

"What a travesty—can you imagine dying in a suit like that?"

"No, some idiot ghostwrites my tweets."

"I could feel my taste buds being manipulated."

"It's good, but I don't know if it's refrigerator door good."

"Please. Have you any idea what goes in those survival meals?"

"I blame all the violent cave paintings."

"No, as a matter of fact, I don't want to rate it on a scale of one to ten."

"You call *this* fake news?"

"Come on in—just throw your coats in the garbage."

"Today I was told my résumé was really absorbent."

CAREER
SUICIDE

S.GROSS

“Food critic from the *Times* is here.”

"You're right—things are funnier in threes."

"We have to start over. God shot down Noah's design concept."

"I don't want a refund—I want two hours of my life back!"

Contributors

David Borchart (18, 30, 77, 116) is a cartoonist for the *New Yorker*, and his cartoons have appeared in *Esquire* and *Time* magazine. His serial cartoon *A Prisoner of Ghoul Island* can be seen online at ghoulisland.com.

Pat Byrnes (29, 52, 87, 94) has been a cartoonist for the *New Yorker* since 1998 and is a winner of the National Cartoonist Society's Best Gag Cartoonist of the Year (2017). Previous careers include voice actor, ad copywriter, and aerospace engineer.

Roz Chast (49, 79) is an award winning *New Yorker* cartoonist and *New York Times* bestselling author. Her new book is *Going Into Town: A Love Letter to New York*.

Frank Cotham (92) sold his first cartoon to the *New Yorker* in 1993. Since then he has sold over 750 cartoons to the magazine. His work can be seen at the Cartoon Bank (cartoonbank.com).

Matt Diffee (72, 78, 105, 129) is a cartoonist among other things. His book *Hand Drawn Jokes for Smart Attractive People* isn't for everyone.

Liza Donnelly (22, 73) is an award winning cartoonist and writer for the *New Yorker* and is resident cartoonist at CBS News. Donnelly's book *Women On Men* was a finalist for the Thurber Prize for American Humor; and her history of women cartoonists, *Funny Ladies: The New Yorker's Women Cartoonists*, is considered a resource for historians.

Nick Downes's (43, 61, 65, 71, 75, 82, 91, 96, 100, 112, 115, 119, 124, 128, 139) work has appeared in many magazines in both the US and UK. He has had published two collections of his cartoons, as well a successful line of irreverent, rather subversive, greeting cards.

Bob Eckstein (24, 44, 59, 64, 76, 85, 125) is a snowman expert (see *The Illustrated History of the Snowman*) and a *New York Times* bestselling author. His work can be seen at bobeckstein.com and he can be followed @Bob_Eckstein.

Liana Finck's (58) work appears regularly in the *New Yorker*. Her most recent graphic novel is *Passing for Human*, published by Random House in 2018.

Mort Gerberg (8, 50) is a cartoonist and author whose work has appeared in magazines, newspapers, books, online, home videos, film, and television. It can be seen at mortgerberg.com.

Alex Gregory (17, 37, 42, 51, 67, 90, 108, 110, 137) is a Hollywood screenwriter. His work can be seen at the Cartoon Bank (cartoonbank.com).

Sam Gross (21, 27, 62, 83, 101, 109, 135) has created around thirty thousand cartoons. He has published many cartoon books and was the cartoon editor for *National Lampoon*, *Smoke*, and *Parents* magazine.

William Haefeli's (12, 25, 33, 35, 66, 118, 126) cartoons have been appearing in the *New Yorker* since 1998. He lives in Los Angeles.

Sid Harris (60, 113) has published thousands of cartoons. Many of them can be seen at sciencecartoonsplus.com.

Bruce Eric Kaplan (14, 39, 47, 55, 81, 102, 132) is a cartoonist for the *New Yorker* and a television writer and producer.

Edward Koren (16, 117, 121) has contributed to the *New Yorker* since 1962. He has been a Guggenheim Fellow and was Vermont's Cartoonist Laureate from 2015 to 2018.

Ken Krimstein (28, 45) is a cartoonist, graphic novelist, writer, and 3.5 level tennis player. In 2018 he published *The Three Escapes of Hannah Arendt: A Tyranny of Truth*. You can see more of his work at kenkrimstein.com

Robert Leighton (13, 84, 103) (robert-leighton.com) has been contributing to the *New Yorker* since 2002. As a puzzle-writer, he cowrote *The New Yorker Book of Cartoon Puzzles and Games*.

Bob Mankoff (20, 32, 80, 95) has published over 950 cartoons in the *New Yorker* magazine where he was cartoon editor for twenty years. He is now the cartoon and humor editor at *Esquire* magazine.

Patricia Marx (49), staff writer for the *New Yorker*, was a writer for *Saturday Night Live* and *Rugrats*, and is the author of several books. Her new book is *Why Don't You Write My Eulogy Now So I Can Correct It?*, illustrated by Roz Chast. Marx was the first woman elected to the *Harvard Lampoon* and has taught screenwriting and humor writing at Princeton. She was a 2015 Guggenheim Fellowship recipient.

Michael Maslin (11, 56, 74, 98) began contributing to the *New Yorker* in 1977. His website, *Ink Spill*, is devoted to *New Yorker* cartoonists and cartoons.

The Surreal McCoy's (106) work can be seen at thesurrealmccoy.com and is featured in *The Inking Woman: 250 Years of Women Cartoon and Comic Artists in Britain*. *The Wolf of Baghdad: A Memoir of a Lost Homeland* (2020) is her first graphic memoir.

Steve McGinn (68) appears regularly in *Funny Times*, and his *Toons by Stev-o* appears daily online. He was formerly the editorial page cartoonist at the *Beacon Hill Times*. He can be followed at @toonsbystevo.

Paul Noth (54) is a staff cartoonist for the *New Yorker* magazine, where his work has appeared regularly since 2004. He has written for *Late Night with Conan O'Brien* and was an animation consultant for *Saturday Night Live.* He is the author of the middle-grade novels *How to Sell Your Family to the Aliens* and *How to Properly Dispose of Planet Earth*. His work can be seen at paulnoth.com.

John O'Brien's (41) work can be found in many publications including the *New Yorker*, and in over one hundred children's books. He can be found living in South Jersey or at johnobrienillustrator.com.

Teresa Burns Parkhurst's (133) cartoons have been published in a number of magazines, most recently in the *New Yorker*, and with several greeting card companies. She is both proud and ashamed to have been counted among the Usual Gang of Idiots at *MAD* magazine since 2003. She enjoys not going places.

Danny Shanahan (9, 53) has had more than 1,200 cartoons and a dozen covers published in the *New Yorker*, as well many other publications, including *Esquire*, *Fortune*, *Playboy*, and the *New York Times*. He has published four anthologies of his work and has appeared in dozens of *New Yorker* collections. He lives in Rhinebeck, New York.

Michael Shaw (26, 86, 136) has contributed cartoons to the *New Yorker* since 1999. Further proof of his peculiar cartooning efforts can be found at myshawrona.com.

Barbara Smaller's (40, 107, 127, 130) cartoons have appeared in numerous publications, anthologies and, since 1996, regularly in the *New Yorker*. She is currently working on a book based on drawings from her *Course of Empire* series that has been featured in the *New Yorker's* Daily Shouts.

Edward Steed (15) has been a cartoonist for the *New Yorker* since 2013.

Mick Stevens (7, 36, 46, 70, 89, 93, 99, 122, 131, 134, 138) has been drawing cartoons for the *New Yorker* for over thirty-five years. His books include *A Mystery, Wrapped in an Enigma, Served on a Bed of Lettuce*; *If Ducks Carried Guns*; and *Things Not to do Today* and a newer e-book called *I Really Should Be Drawing: The Blook*, available online.

Julia Suits (63) is a *New Yorker* cartoonist and freelance illustrator. She lives in Austin, Texas. To see more of her projects, visit juliasuits.net.

Mark Thompson (31) has been a *New Yorker* cartoon contributor since 2008 and lives in the Twin Cities area.

P.C. Vey's (10, 88, 97, 111) cartoons regularly appear in the *New Yorker*. His work also has been published in *Harvard Business Review*, *Barron's*, *National Lampoon*, the *Wall Street Journal*, the *New York Times*, *Prospect*, *Playboy*, *AARP Bulletin*, and the *Boston Globe*. He has had three collections of cat cartoons published by Penguin/Plume and has contributed to many books of cartoons on a variety of subjects.

Kim Warp (123) began contributing to the *New Yorker* in 1999 and is a winner of the National Cartoonist's Society's Best Gag Cartoonist of the Year (2000). She frequently contributes the *New Yorker's* Daily Cartoon.

Christopher Weyant (19, 23, 34, 57, 69, 104, 114) is a cartoonist for the *New Yorker* and an editorial cartoonist for the *Boston Globe*. In 2015, he won the Theodor Seuss Geisel Award for his picture book, *You Are (Not) Small*, written by Anna Kang. Follow him at christopherweyant.com and on Instagram @christopherweyant.

Jack Ziegler (38, 48, 120) was a cartoonist for the *New Yorker* magazine from 1974 to 2017. During his lifetime he produced over 24,000 cartoons, and sold over 3,000, mainly to the *New Yorker.* You can find his work at jackziegler.com

Acknowledgments

Thank you to all the contributing artists. Special thanks to those who also participated on panels at book events: Barbara Smaller, Edward Koren, Liza Donnelly, and Danny Shanahan. That group also includes friends Nick Downes, Robert Leighton, Sam Gross, Michael Maslin, and David Borchart, who not only did panels but also provided invaluable feedback and help for the book. I want to thank Trevor Hoey of Cartoon Collections and Jaylen Amaker of the Cartoon Bank for all their time and assistance for the book.

Thanks to my wife Tamar Stone, who is very involved in my books, and my agent Joy Tutela for finding a home for this special series. And a big thank-you to Kristen, Rob, Wes, Paul, and the rest of the Princeton Architectural Press team.

—*Bob Eckstein*

Published by
Princeton Architectural Press
202 Warren Street
Hudson, New York 12534
www.papress.com

Printed and bound in China
23 22 21 20 4 3 2 1 First edition

ISBN: 978-1-61689-853-3

Editor: Kristen Hewitt
Series design: Paul Wagner
Design assistance: Paula Baver

Front cover: Danny Shanahan
Back cover: Bob Eckstein

Special thanks to: Janet Behning, Abby Bussel, Jan Cigliano Hartman, Susan Hershberg, Stephanie Holstein, Lia Hunt, Valerie Kamen, Cooper Lippert, Jennifer Lippert, Sara McKay, Parker Menzimer, Wes Seeley, Rob Shaeffer, Sara Stemen, Jessica Tackett, Marisa Tesoro, and Joseph Weston of Princeton Architectural Press
—Kevin C. Lippert, publisher

For permission to reprint cartoons, on pages listed, we gratefully thank the cartoonists of the following publications:
American Bystander, 44
Barron's, 10, 19, 23–24, 34, 57, 64, 69, 100, 112, 124, 128, 139
MAD magazine, 76
New Yorker, 7–9, 12, 14–17, 20–22, 25, 27, 30, 32–33, 35–39, 42, 47–51, 54–55, 58–59, 62, 66–67, 72–73, 78–81, 83–85, 90, 92, 95, 101–102, 104–105, 108–110, 116–117, 120–122, 132, 134–135, 137
The Oldie, 43, 61, 65, 75, 82, 87, 115, 119, 129
Prospect, 88
The Spectator, 71, 91

Library of Congress Cataloging-in-Publication Data available upon request.

RONE IN
GEELONG

Cover front:
Rone
Without Darkness There is No Light (Dark) 2021
RONE in Geelong (Douglass Gallery installation)
Geelong Gallery
Photographer: Rone

Cover back:
Rone
Without Darkness There is No Light (Light) 2021
RONE in Geelong (Douglass Gallery installation)
Geelong Gallery
Photographer: Rone

Geelong Gallery

Little Malop Street
Geelong VIC 3220 Australia
T +61 3 5229 3645
info@geelonggallery.org.au

geelonggallery.org.au

Government partners

CREATIVE VICTORIA

RONE in Geelong

Geelong presenting partners

Events Geelong

gh COMMERCIAL
Flooring Solutions

Major partner

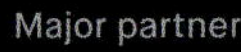

RONE in Geelong
Geelong Gallery
27 February to 16 May 2021

Curator
Lisa Sullivan
Senior Curator, Geelong Gallery

ISBN
978-1-875237-27-2

Publisher
Geelong Gallery, 2021

Catalogue design
Pidgeon Ward

Typeset in
Maison Neue and MFred

Production and printing
Adams Print

Stock
Knight Vellum (cover)
and Satin Art

Print run
2250

Image reproductions
Rone: all works and documentary photographs are reproduced courtesy of Rone (unless otherwise stated).

Geelong Gallery collection works: copyright holders are attributed in image captions (where applicable).

Photography
Survey works:
Rone, Lloyd Knowles, Matthew Stanton

CONTENTS

FOREWORD/ ACKNOWLEDGEMENTS

JASON SMITH
DIRECTOR & CEO
GEELONG GALLERY

RONE in Geelong
(installation view, Geelong Gallery, 2021)
Photographer: Tony Mott

RONE in Geelong is one of the most ambitiously scaled art projects presented by Geelong Gallery, and is the outcome of an exceptionally productive collaboration between the artist, his creative team, the entire staff of the Gallery, and our numerous supporting partners.

It is a pleasure to celebrate artists for whom Geelong is a place of special significance. As someone who was raised in Geelong, Tyrone Wright's commitment to realising an extraordinary, immersive installation in Geelong Gallery is a testament to his enduring sense of home.

I thank Tyrone for entrusting the Gallery with the presentation of the first survey of his remarkable practice over the past two decades, and for his labour intensive, lengthy undertaking to wonderfully transform our Douglass Gallery. Tyrone's response to some of the riches of our collection has inspired a close and creative dialogue with the exhibition's curator Lisa Sullivan, and I thank Lisa for her insightful and scholarly interpretation of Rone's mesmerising and affecting art.

I want to acknowledge the sheer hard work and professionalism of members of Tyrone's creative production team, and thank Alice Goulter, Sandra Powell, Andrew King, Carly Spooner, Nick Batterham, Callum Preston, Mo Wyse, and Hannah Marshall.

In addition to works borrowed from the artist's personal collection, I thank lenders to the survey exhibition including Paul Bell, Sharyn Lowe, Callum Preston, The SANDREW Collection, Josh Walker, and a private collector.

Additionally, I thank Geelong Contemporary and Adelaide Brighton Limited, both of which have supported the acquisition of works by Rone for the Gallery's collection.

Our Presenting partners have been crucial to our realisation of a project of this scale. I warmly thank the City of Greater Geelong, who through Mayor Stephanie Asher, and Deputy Mayor Trent Sullivan, provide ongoing support of Geelong Gallery's purpose to provide an experience of art that enriches peoples' lives.

I thank our additional Presenting partners: Events Geelong and Sharon Cockerell, Executive Officer. GH Commercial has provided essential major support and I thank John Harrison, National Marketing Manager.

Our Major partner is Visit Victoria (Regional Events) and I thank The Hon. Martin Pakula, Minister for Tourism, Sport and Major Events, and Monique George, Manager Regional Events Fund.

I warmly thank our Exhibition partners: Mercedes Benz Geelong, Mr Moto/Drawcard, V/Line, Port Phillip Ferries, Central Geelong Marketing, and EL&C Baillieu. Your support is most appreciated.

The commitment of our Learn partners is essential for the reach of this exhibition to students of all ages, and I thank The Pierce Armstrong Foundation, and the Museum of Play and Art (MOPA).

The Design Files is a valued Media partner, and we also thank Geelong Surf Coast Living and Provincial Media for their ongoing support.

I am most grateful to our Publication partner, the Gordon Darling Foundation and thank the Trustees and Alister Shew, Administrator, for his assistance. This beautiful publication is again the work of David Pidgeon and Lachlan Mason of Pidgeon Ward, and Shane Soutar and the team at Adams Print. Thank you all.

The staff of Geelong Gallery deserve special thanks for their unwavering commitment to ensuring the complex but seamless delivery of this major exhibition, and especially as so much of the project's planning needed to be resolved through the uncertainties of 2020. I would like to mention in particular the meticulous planning work of Pip Minney, Exhibitions Manager, and John Stabb, Building & Spaces Coordinator. I also acknowledge Penny Whitehead, Deputy Director—Development & Commercial Operations.

In this 125th anniversary year of the establishment of Geelong Gallery I thank Tyrone Wright for his thought-provoking contribution to the exhibition history of this great institution.

WITHOUT DARKNESS THERE IS NO LIGHT

LISA SULLIVAN
SENIOR CURATOR
GEELONG GALLERY

RONE in Geelong: in progress
(Geelong Gallery, 2021)
Photographer: Tony Mott

'How sad it is!' murmured Dorian Gray, with his eyes still fixed upon his own portrait. 'How sad it is! I shall grow old, and horrible, and dreadful. But this picture will remain always young. It will never be older than this particular day … If it were only the other way! If it were I who was always to be young, and the picture that was to grow old! For that—for that—I would give everything! Yes, there is nothing in the whole world I would not give! I would give my soul for that!'[1]

Oscar Wilde
The Picture of Dorian Gray, 1891

In his desire to retain his youthful beauty, the main protagonist in Oscar Wilde's late-nineteenth century novel *The Picture of Dorian Gray* makes a Faustian-pact. In doing so, his painted portrait comes to represent his soul, the picture's monstrousness reflecting Gray's dissolute life and murderous actions. The portrait becomes a hideous but true representation of its subject while the artifice of Gray's seemingly eternal youth is retained as the decades pass. In the final pages, Gray's attempt to destroy the painting brings about his own death: his aged body discovered alongside the now redeemed portrait of the beautiful youth.

Wilde's narrative explores the ambition and the power of portraiture to capture the essence of a subject, and in doing so elaborates on the dichotomies of beauty and ugliness, youth and old age, and goodness and evil. *The Picture of*

Oppositions, dichotomies, and portraiture are fundamental to the practice of Geelong-born artist Rone. His works are about beauty and decay, the enduring and the obsolete, the permanent and the ephemeral. And in his site-specific installation for Geelong Gallery, he gives material form to darkness and light in portraits painted on opposite walls of a vast gallery. It is the same female subject, in one rendition bathed in luminosity, in the other emerging from darkness. They symbolise what Wilde ascribes to Dorian Gray as 'the terrible pleasure of a double life'.[2]

In painting these portraits at a gigantic scale, Rone intends that they preside over the space he has conceived for them: a grand reception room from an earlier time. This human presence is a crucial element of Rone's installations that transform existing, often derelict buildings. It alludes to the ways in which we inhabit spaces; the residues of our presence; the memories that we hold of our experiences of certain spaces; and the ways in which we might haunt and be haunted by places.

In the gallery, Rone's portraits are youthful representations that adhere to concepts of feminine beauty. It is the room itself that has deteriorated over time, abandoned with few signs of its former glory, and only suggestions of what might have brought about its dereliction.

CAT. NO. 19
The Lobby (Empire) 2019
archival pigment print
on 310 gsm Canson Baryta; A/P
Collection of the artist
Photographer: Rone

Once prized paintings are now blackened by soot, and their frames are in various states of disrepair; items of furniture wear signs of neglect, decay and damage; once lustrous ceiling fabrics are soiled through exposure to the rain and leaves that have entered the building through broken skylights; the elaborately decorated carpet is stained and worn; and layers of dust accumulate on surfaces. A musical score evokes sounds that would have once rung through this room, now lost to time and assuming a melancholic, haunting strain. The guests for whom the music played are long gone.

In recent years Rone has built a reputation for the exceptional transformation of abandoned spaces, into which he constructs rich narratives and evocative sensory experiences. Most recently, Rone's epically scaled project *Empire* (2019) overtook Burnham Beeches, the grand Art Deco residence in the Dandenong Ranges **(CAT. NOS 19-22)**. With a team of collaborators, Rone transformed the unoccupied mansion to create an experiential journey through twelve rooms, with transitions and changes to reflect the seasons. Linking each space was the haunting large-scale portrait of a woman: her identity was unknown, and her link to the building unclear, but her persistent presence in each of the rooms provoked visitors to imagine her personal story—a life lived at the height of the mansion's heyday.

Opposing forces and inevitable change were also conditioned in Rone's *Alpha Project* and *Omega Project* (2017). In the Greek alphabet 'Alpha' and 'Omega' represent the first and the last. In the Book of Revelation of the Christian Bible they signify the beginning and the end. The installation *Alpha* was completed in the former machine rooms of the decommissioned Alphington Paper Mill—the site of Victoria's first paper mill—ahead of its demolition and the redevelopment of the site. *Omega* was staged in a derelict Federation-era weatherboard cottage neighbouring the Mill. In their distinct settings, the two projects effectively encompassed the dichotomies of work and home, industry and leisure, and beauty and decay.

In the partially demolished industrial building Rone completed five murals, exploiting the Mill's monumental scale and the raw material qualities of the remaining structure. The murals documented in *Above This*, 2017 **(CAT. NO. 14)** and *Without Darkness There is No Light*, 2017 **(CAT. NO. 15)** came into being through an initial process of removal: the artist removed layers of grime built up over a century of operations, exposing brickwork and enabling him to paint the tonal range that gives form to the portraits. That all that remains of Rone's project, and the Mill itself, are photographs printed on paper is poignant.

CAT. NO. 15
Without Darkness There is No Light (Alpha Project) (detail) 2017
archival pigment print
on 310 gsm Canson Baryta; A/P
Collection of the artist
Photographer: Rone

CAT. NO. 16
The Blue Room (Omega Project) 2017
archival pigment print
on 310 gsm Canson Baryta; A/P
Collection of the artist
Photographer: Rone

Photo-documentation of his ephemeral site-specific installations has increasingly become an essential aspect of Rone's practice, and is a strategy that links to his origins in street art. According to Rone:

> *The concept of creating something beautiful within the context of decay and decline is central to the experience of any street artist. As is the idea that whatever you create might be gone the next day. For the artist, street art is all about embracing that transience and impermanence ... Because it's often so short-lived, street art tends to exist more through the ways that people document it; through photographs, prints and social media.*[3]

While the darkened palette of *Alpha* reflected the industrial history of the paper mill, in the weatherboard house in which *Omega* was set, Rone and collaborator Carly Spooner introduced softer, more 'domestic' colours and a range of homely furnishings and fittings that heightened a feeling of nostalgia. *The Blue Room*, 2017 **(CAT. NO. 16)** and *The Green Room*, 2017 **(CAT. NO. 17)** reconfigure a bedroom and an informal dining room to recall 1950s suburbia: a chenille bedspread, a typical dressing table, a Laminex table, plastic flowers, and the now kitsch swan vases. The portrait of a young woman again recurs through the home, her visage appearing on damaged walls, above rubble-strewn floors and beneath mildewed ceilings. For *RONE in Geelong*, the artist has recreated *The Green Room* in a three-dimensional tableau, effectively bringing previous photo-documentation to three-dimensional life. Rone's work plays with time. He conceptually distorts it here through the re-materialisation of something that was demolished soon after it was created in 2017.

Rone's installation for Geelong Gallery extends the artist's practice through his response to the building's early-twentieth century architecture, and to works of art. Rone has researched and mined the Gallery's collection, connecting with decorative arts, painted portraits, watercolour landscapes, and the first major work acquired by Geelong Gallery in 1900—Frederick McCubbin's *A bush burial* (1890). The Gallery's invitation to Rone initiated a profound re-engagement with a collection and an institution that he visited in the formative years of his life growing up in Geelong.

Above top:
Alexander Webb
On the You Yangs 1870–89
watercolour and ink
Geelong Gallery
Purchased 1995

Above:
Hans Heysen
Gum trees in Flinders Ranges 1936
watercolour over pencil
Geelong Gallery
Gift of Mr and Mrs Brian Baulch and family in memory of Mr and Mrs SS Baulch through the Australian Government's Cultural Gifts Program, 2011
Photographer: George Stawicki

Frederick McCubbin
A bush burial 1890
oil on canvas
Geelong Gallery
Purchased by public subscription, 1900
Photographer: Andrew Curtis

The unique aspect of *RONE in Geelong* is the artist's and his team's meticulous creation of scaled reproductions of works from the collection for the interior setting. While the artist's reputation for working in abandoned spaces and sites of imminent demolition may seem at odds with a gallery's structural permanence and its *raison d'être* to preserve visual culture, Rone's installation provokes new thinking on the very idea of the museum: of the images and objects that help shape collective cultural memory; of the things we value as signs of our lives and times; and of what can so easily be lost.

The installation's general colour scheme takes its lead from early 20th century ceramics by Geelong-born artist Florence Royce. In the early 1900s, Royce offered private classes in china painting along with watercolour painting and stencilling, whilst also teaching ceramics at Geelong's Gordon Technical College. In 1939 her students gifted a selection of her works to the Gallery and these were augmented decades later through the bequest of local collector Dorothy McAllister. Royce decorated traditional vases, bowls, platters, and cups and saucers—often blanks from manufacturers—with designs incorporating Australian flora and fauna, and non-Indigenous flowers, in a muted palette predominantly of greens, blues and pinks. The subtlety of Royce's colour range also informed Rone's selection of watercolours from the collection.

Since its acquisition, McCubbin's *A bush burial* has assumed an iconic status. Generations of visitors to Geelong Gallery—including Rone in his youth—have been captivated by McCubbin's colonial bush narrative in which an unidentified pioneer is laid to rest, while his grieving wife and child stand beside his grave.

The powerfully affecting sense of loss and melancholy that pervades McCubbin's scene leads us to defining characteristics of Rone's oeuvre: his works reflect on absence, memory, and what remains after a life is lived. Rone's elaborate *mise-en-scène* draw on the traditions of *vanitas* or *memento mori*—that genre of still life painting in which objects such as skulls, candles, timepieces, fruit, flowers, and insects symbolise the futility and folly of earthly pleasures, humankind's transience, and the inevitability of death. In then photographing these installations, Rone compounds his memorialisation. As Susan Sontag wrote in *On Photography*: 'All photographs are *memento mori*. To take a photograph is to participate in another person's (or thing's) mortality, vulnerability, mutability. Precisely by slicing out this moment and freezing it, all photographs testify to time's relentless melt.'[4]

Rone also employs the venerable tradition of *trompe l'oeil* painting in the installation's wall finishes, plaster tondo reliefs, and decorative architectural panels. *Trompe l'oeil* translates as 'deceive the eye' and has long been associated with painting that intentionally seeks to trick the viewer—if only momentarily—into mistaking a two-dimensional representation for three-dimensional reality. Its origins date as far back as 400AD when Roman author Pliny the Elder recounted the story of a competition between two artists, Zeuxis and Parrhasios, who sought to deceive each other through their painting skills.

Florence Royce
Cup and saucer 1930–50
Large bowl c. 1930s
Fruit dish 1930–50
hand-painted porcelain with gilt edging
Geelong Gallery
Bequest of Dorothy McAllister, 1987
Photographer: Andrew Curtis

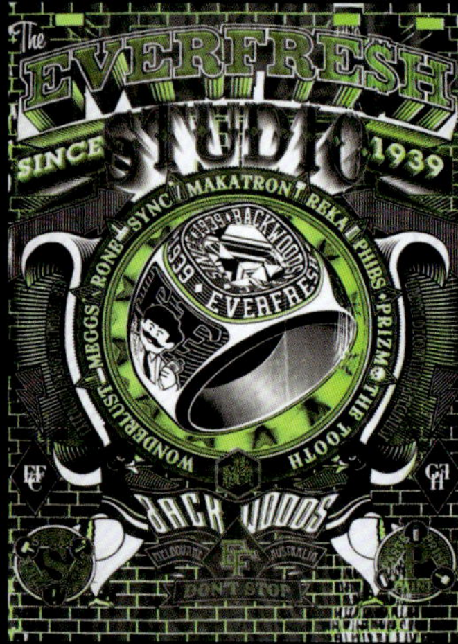

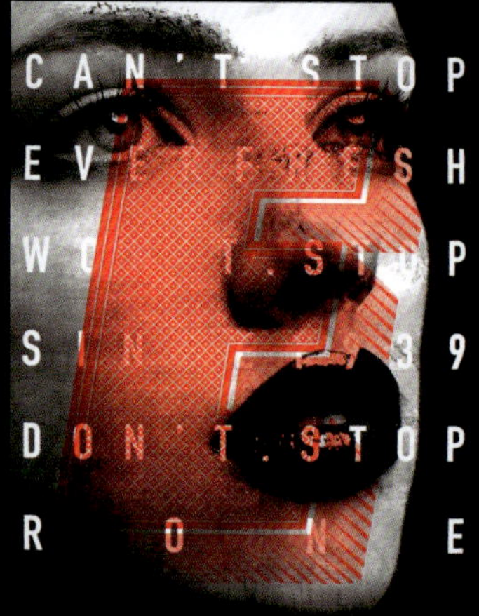

Posters 2011
screenprints
Collection of the artist

A 100-year-old *trompe l'oeil* painting was the centrepiece of Rone's first large-scale public project, *Empty*, presented in the former Star Lyric Theatre in Fitzroy in late 2016. Opened in 1911, the Star Lyric Theatre was one of Melbourne's first silent movie cinemas: its 'screen' wall featured a *trompe l'oeil* mural simulating circular windows, the Star Lyric banner and decorative plasterwork. In preparing the wall's surface for a large-scale mural, Rone uncovered remnants of the *trompe l'oeil* painting which were then re-painted and integrated into the final portrait composition. *Empty* also included photographs of more intimately scaled projects—murals painted in derelict and abandoned homes such as *I've Seen Fire and I've Seen Rain*, 2016 **(CAT. NO. 12)**—and portraits painted on canvas.

Well before the Star Lyric Theatre installation, Rone's canvases and works on paper incorporated aspects of *trompe l'oeil*. In 2011 he designed and screen-printed several posters—four of which had a centrally placed letter representing those in his name—that were intended to simulate mass-produced promotional posters pasted on the street. Evolving from his own practice of paste-ups, these posters drew on the designs and rapid messaging of street posters promoting music gigs, concerts, or clothing sales, and were printed in high volume on low quality paper stock. The posters became the 'ground' for works, pasted in multiple layers onto canvases and boards and prematurely aged in the studio to appear as they might if exposed to the elements on the street. Works such as *L'Inconnue de la Rue*, 2011 **(CAT. NO. 7)**, *Pain and Guilt (i)*, 2011 **(CAT. NO. 8)**, and *Blue Horizon*, 2015 **(CAT. NO. 10)**, reveal this layering and ageing process, with remnants of the posters visible beneath portraits. In *Forget the Past, You Can Only Change the Future*, 2014 **(CAT. NO. 9)**, Rone also incorporates fragments of wallpaper, a development that foreshadowed the transformation of domestic environments in projects such as *Omega* and *Empire*.

Rone's engagement with the Geelong Gallery collection included a selection of female portraits such as *Mrs Margaret McArthur of Meningoort* (1856–57) by Robert Dowling, *Portrait of Mrs Hugh Chambers and her daughter Hester* (1853) by Marshall Claxton, George Lambert's *The black hat* (1920s), *Portrait of Betty Paterson* (1939) by her sister Esther Paterson, and William Dargie's *Portrait of the artist's wife* (1940).

CAT. NO. 8
Pain and Guilt (i) 2011
stencilled spray enamel
and acrylic polymer emulsion
on screen-printed paper
The SANDREW Collection
Photographer: Matthew Stanton

Spanning almost a century, the paintings reflect stylistic developments in the portrait genre, the evolution of representations of women which could be said to reflect their changing role in society, and the telling relationship between subjects and artist. Images of the female subject—the female muse—have predominated in Rone's visual lexicon since the emergence of the first 'Jane Doe' in 2004, stencilled on the streets of Melbourne. At that time, Rone's motivation was to counter the hyper-masculine imagery that dominated street art, and his subject emerged from the pages of a magazine.

The face of the anonymous 'Jane Doe' became a signature image in Rone's oeuvre, transitioning from stencils/paper cuts **(CAT. NO. 2)**, to large paper paste-ups, to multi-poster configurations. *Suzanne*, 2010 **(CAT. NO. 6)** similarly emerged from a random photograph from the 1970s, however in recent years Rone has introduced a more direct engagement with his subjects, photographing models to create reference images for canvas works, large-scale outdoor murals and various installations.

Beyond Rone's site-specific installation in Geelong, the Hitchcock Gallery is hung with 19th century works from the Gallery's collection, amongst which a selection of the original works that Rone has reproduced are hung. These insertions act as an *aide-mémoire*, linking the copy and the original and juxtaposing the world of fantasy with reality. This simple curatorial act of mirroring recalls Wilde's narrative, with Dorian's portrait representing a reflection of his soul.

The antithetical positions that Rone and Wilde variously present—beauty and decay, youth and ageing, good and evil, truth and fiction, and darkness and light—highlight that one position rarely exists without the other. In the preface to *The Picture of Dorian Gray* Wilde writes:

> *All art is at once surface and symbol.*
> *Those who go beneath the surface*
> *do so at their peril.*
> *Those who read the symbol do*
> *so at their peril.*
> *It is the spectator, and not life,*
> *that art really mirrors.*

Rone invites us to venture beyond the surface and to engage with the deeper meaning of his installations, and in doing so highlights that in the human experience without darkness, there is no light.

CAT. NO. 2
Jane Doe 2005
paper cut
Collection of the artist
Photographer: Lloyd Knowles

CAT. NO. 6
Suzanne 2010
stencil on canvas
The SANDREW Collection
Photographer: Matthew Stanton

ENDNOTES

1 Oscar Wilde, *The Picture of Dorian Gray*, Penguin Books, United Kingdom, 1957, p. 33.
2 Wilde, p. 194.
3 Rone, 'Omega Project', 2020, viewed 4 November 2020, r-o-n-e.com/omega-project
4 Susan Sontag, *On Photography*, Rosetta Books, New York, 1973, p. 11.
5 As reported in *The Argus*, 6 November 1911, the Star Lyric Theatre opened on Saturday 4 November with one of the opening night's films being a version of *Faust*. *Trove*, viewed 12 November 2020, nla.gov.au/nla.news-article1 1629737

THE INST

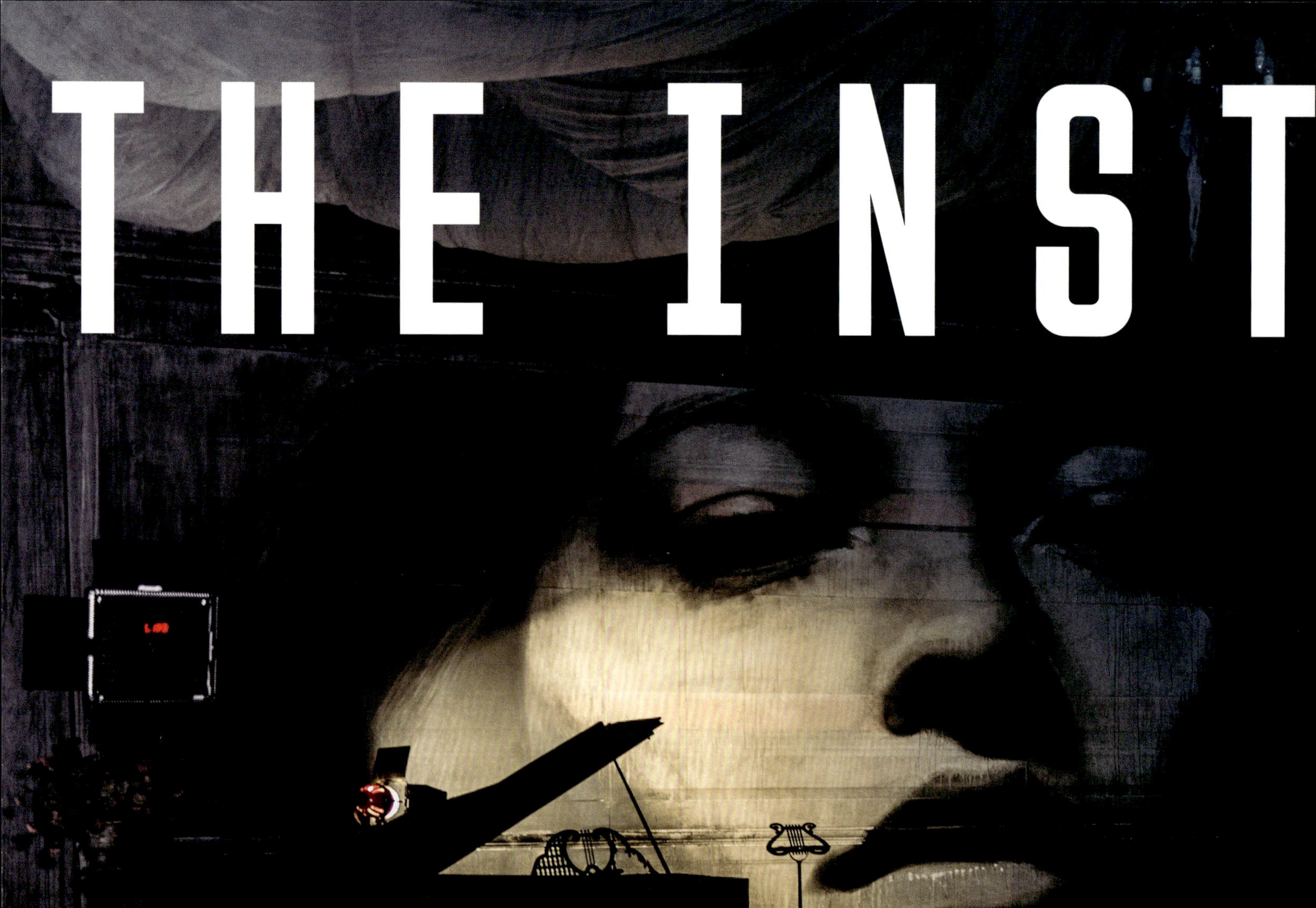

ALLATION

Previous pages:
RONE in Geelong: in progress
(Geelong Gallery, 2021)
Photographer: Tony Mott

Rone
Without Darkness There is No Light (Light) 2021
(*RONE in Geelong*, Douglass Gallery installation, Geelong Gallery)
archival pigment print on Canson Baryta 310 gsm; A/P
Courtesy of the artist
Photographer: Rone

Rone
Without Darkness There is No Light (Dark) 2021
(*RONE in Geelong*, Douglass Gallery installation, Geelong Gallery)
archival pigment print on Canson Baryta 310 gsm; A/P
Courtesy of the artist
Photographer: Rone

Above:
Douglass Gallery
(installation view including works by John Scurry, Grace Cossington Smith, Margaret Preston, Godfrey Miller, John Brack, Nicholas Mangan, Rosalie Gascoigne and Albert Tucker, Geelong Gallery, 2021)
Photographer: Andrew Curtis

Opposite:
Rone
Without Darkness There is No Light (Light) (detail) 2021
(*RONE in Geelong*, Douglass Gallery installation, Geelong Gallery)
archival pigment print on Canson Baryta 310 gsm; A/P
Courtesy of the artist
Photographer: Rone

Above:
Douglass Gallery
(installation view including works by Arthur Boyd and Adam Pyett, Geelong Gallery, 2021)
Arthur Boyd's works reproduced with the permission of Bundanon Trust
Photographer: Andrew Curtis

Opposite:
Rone
Without Darkness There is No Light (Dark) (detail) 2021
(*RONE in Geelong*, Douglass Gallery installation, Geelong Gallery)
archival pigment print on Canson Baryta 310 gsm; A/P
Courtesy of the artist
Photographer: Rone

THE MAKING OF

TYRONE WRIGHT

All photographs reproduced in *The Making Of* and *Behind the Music: RONE in Geelong: in progress* (Melbourne studio and Geelong Gallery, featuring Rone and collaborators Carly Spooner and Callum Preston, 2021) Photographers: Tony Mott, Rone

In early 2019, my photograph *I've Seen Fire and I've Seen Rain* (2016) from the *Empty* series was acquired for the Geelong Gallery collection with the support of the fundraising group Geelong Contemporary. Being represented in an institutional collection in my hometown was a significant career milestone, and soon after, an invitation to exhibit at the Gallery was received.

SANDREW (consultants Sandra Powell and Andrew King) and I began a conversation with Geelong Gallery for a potential project in 2020, given much of 2019 was occupied with the *Empire* project. Initial ideas included a survey of my work, but the proposal for a new installation was also discussed. We thought about transforming a nearby abandoned house as an offsite project or moving sections of a house into the Gallery. We started to think about the Gallery itself. Could we make *it* the site for an installation?

The uniqueness of the building presented numerous logistical challenges, including the limited amount of time the allocated space could be closed to the public for installation, and the requirement to return the space to its original, pristine state

The first idea was to paint the walls in the Douglass Gallery; however, we couldn't achieve this in only a few weeks. We then came up with a plan to paint the walls on panels that would then be installed over existing walls, giving me considerably more time to create the work. Fortuitously, I was given access to a huge warehouse in Melbourne where we built a full-sized replica of the Douglass Gallery so we could hang panels, paint them and set the scene to see how it would all come together (for an exhibition that had, by then, been postponed until early 2021 due to COVID-19).

The second major aspect of the project was the floor. I wanted visitors to feel transported when they entered the space. I knew how I was going to transform the walls, but the Gallery's shiny, pristine floorboards presented a new challenge. Interior stylist Carly Spooner and I consulted references from an old film for floor designs that looked like they were painted. We looked far and wide for a similar carpet, or even rugs, but the Douglass Gallery has 230 square metres of floor to cover. The idea of a custom-printed carpet was made possible when Geelong-based company GH Commercial generously agreed to sponsor the project.

I set to work creating a design that could be produced as a digitally printed carpet. We could now cover the entire floor and create a distressed finish to fulfill the vision of a grand reception room, using a new carpet that looks faded and stained by years of neglect.

The theme of the grand reception room was inspired by a trip to Venice in late 2019, where I often found the *trompe l'oeil* painting within interiors more beautiful, or more dramatic, than the actual marbles and moulded plaster details. I'm not sure if the faux effects of 2-D *trompe l'oeil* show a craftsmanship that can be lost in the production of the three-dimensional forms, or whether paint better represents what it seeks to imitate. But for me, showing an illusion of what could be is sometimes more exciting than what is. My work hints at what could be or what could have been; something I try to exaggerate within each space I work.

Researching the Gallery's collection, I happened upon Florence Royce's works. I loved the muted tones of her painted ceramics. They spoke to what I often try to represent: a fading beauty. Building on the reception room concept, I wanted each end of the room to feel different but to have continuity through the space. Light and dark was the answer to this. The sun-faded colours of the lighter end under the glass ceiling contrasting with the soot-stained darker end of the room, the residue of a burnt piano.

Trompe l'oeil is part of everything I do: the entire space is an illusion. My installations are like a painting that you can walk through. Every object and item in the space has been put there with intent. The objects may not be functional, or even real, but they are representative of the form. This could also be compared to the theatre: a performance of a fictional space where the objects create the narrative.

Many of the items of furniture are replicas; some are easy to spot, but others are simply altered originals.

One example of a replica is the harp made from wood by Callum Preston. The general shape was cut from a few templates and details were added, including strings and a base. I painted the wood gold, then added a patina to age it to fit the era of the room. The harp is a non-functional replica, and the piano is damaged and unplayable, but the musical soundtrack that fills the room, composed by Nick Batterham, is very real.

The idea of replicas also extends to printed reproductions of paintings and watercolours from the Gallery's collection. These were then framed with discarded or second-hand frames so they appear like the originals, only aged and uncared for. The muse, painted directly onto the walls, appears oversized but subtly blends with its surroundings, almost like a form of pareidolia. The muse invites the viewer to engage with the work on a deeper level. We think about other people on an emotional level, differently to the way we might think about objects. Her presence links her to the fabricated history of the space.

FOUR SEASONS
TOTAL LANDSCAPING

T10
T10

TOP LOAD ONLY

BEHIND THE MUSIC

NICK BATTERHAM

The soundtrack to the exhibition is a suite of three pieces of classical music featuring musicians from the Melbourne Symphony Orchestra. In response to Rone's concept of the abandoned function room with its two opposing ends being light and dark, the music features two separate ensembles that play off each other in a musical conversation of layered reflections and repetitions.

At the dark end of the room is the piano, augmented by wind and brass, while at the light end a string quartet plays. Melodies intertwine to form one larger ensemble before receding to their respective ends. The ensembles work both separately and together.

The piano was recorded on an 1897 Schiedmayer & Soehne. Rich in the colourful character of the antique mechanism, its sound emits from the burnt piano at the dark end of the space. It is joined by wind and

At the light end of the room, the strings are mournful and sombre. Within the ensemble, each singular instrument is heard from a different seat at the dining table. The cello at one end, the violin at the other. The viola and bass fill the seats in between.

The suite of three pieces was written at the time of the devastating Black Summer bushfires of 2019–20 and reflects the sadness of these events. *Prelude* establishes the relationship between the solo piano at one end and the cello and viola at the other. *Red Sun Sky* is ominous and brooding: a ten-minute meditation on loss, conjuring the darkened skies, heavy with smoke and the deep crimson sun. As a very slow waltz, it alludes to a past when people danced in the now abandoned reception room. *Dawn Chorus* speaks of new beginnings, the resilience of nature and humanity. From the smallest signs of life, interwoven melodies grow

SURVEY WORKS

RONE

CAT. NO. 1
Untitled 2003
stencil on cardboard
81.0 × 58.0 cm
Collection of the artist
Photographer: Lloyd Knowles

CAT. NO. 2
Jane Doe 2005
paper cut
91.0 × 66.0 cm
Collection of the artist
Photographer: Lloyd Knowles

CAT. NO. 3
Meggs 2007
paper cut
100.0 × 70.0 cm
The SANDREW Collection
Photographer: Matthew Stanton

CAT. NO. 4
The Tooth 2007
paper cut
100.0 × 70.0 cm
On loan from Callum Preston

CAT. NO. 5
Julie (multi-posters) 2010
posters on wood panel
120.0 × 244.0 cm
Collection of the artist
Commissioned by aMBUSH Gallery for Semi Permanent at Melbourne's GPO
Photographer: Lloyd Knowles

CAT. NO. 6
Suzanne 2010
stencil on canvas
123.0 × 91.0 cm
The SANDREW Collection
Photographer: Matthew Stanton

CAT. NO. 7
L'Inconnue de la Rue 2011
stencilled spray enamel and
acrylic polymer emulsion on
screen-printed paper
120.0 × 89.0 cm
The SANDREW Collection
Photographer: Matthew Stanton

CAT. NO. 8
Pain and Guilt (i) 2011
stencilled spray enamel and
acrylic polymer emulsion on
screen-printed paper
120.0 × 89.0 cm
The SANDREW Collection
Photographer: Matthew Stanton

CAT. NO. 9
Forget the Past, You Can Only Change the Future 2014
acrylic polymer emulsion
and mixed media on canvas
300.0 × 250.0 cm
Collection of Sharyn Lowe
Photographer: Matthew Stanton

CAT. NO. 10
Blue Horizon 2015
acrylic polymer emulsion
and mixed media on canvas
200.0 × 150.0 cm
Private collection, Melbourne
Photographer: Matthew Stanton

CAT. NO. 11
Unbreakable 2015
acrylic polymer emulsion
and mixed media on canvas
200.0 × 137.0 cm
Collection of Josh Walker
Photographer: Matthew Stanton

CAT. NO. 12
I've Seen Fire and I've Seen Rain (Empty) 2016
archival pigment print on 310 gsm
Canson Baryta; edition 3 of 3
153.2 × 222.0 cm
Geelong Gallery
Purchased with funds generously
provided by Geelong Contemporary, 2019
Photographer: Rone

CAT. NO. 13
Too Much 2016
acrylic polymer emulsion
and mixed media on canvas
198.5 × 152.5 cm
Collection of Paul Bell
Photographer: Matthew Stanton

CAT. NO. 14
Above This (Alpha Project) 2017
archival pigment print on 310 gsm
Canson Baryta; edition 2 of 5
103.2 × 145.8 cm
Collection of Josh Walker
Photographer: Rone

CAT. NO. 15
Without Darkness There is No Light (Alpha Project) 2017
archival pigment print on 310 gsm
Canson Baryta; A/P
103.2 × 145.8 cm
Collection of the artist
Photographer: Rone

CAT. NO. 16
The Blue Room (Omega Project) 2017
archival pigment print on 310 gsm
Canson Baryta; A/P
103.2 × 145.8 cm
Collection of the artist
Photographer: Rone

CAT. NO. 17
The Green Room (Omega Project) 2017
archival pigment print on 310 gsm
Canson Baryta; A/P
103.2 × 145.8 cm
Collection of the artist
Photographer: Rone

CAT. NO. 18
Geelong Cement Silos 2018
archival pigment print; A/P
103.2 × 145.8 cm
Geelong Gallery
Gift of Adelaide Brighton Limited, 2020
Photographer: Rone

CAT. NO. 19
The Lobby (Empire) 2019
archival pigment print on 310 gsm
Canson Baryta; A/P
144.3 × 101.7 cm
Collection of the artist
Photographer: Rone

CAT. NO. 20
Midnight in the Garden (Empire) 2019
archival pigment print on 310 gsm
Canson Baryta; A/P
103.2 × 145.8 cm
Collection of the artist
Photographer: Rone

CAT. NO. 21
The Music Room (Empire) 2019
archival pigment print on 310 gsm
Canson Baryta; A/P
103.2 × 145.8 cm
Collection of the artist
Photographer: Rone

CAT. NO. 22
The Study (Empire) 2019
archival pigment print on 310 gsm
Canson Baryta; edition 1 of 3
153.2 × 222.0 cm
The SANDREW Collection
Photographer: Rone

CAT. NO. 23
Sub Rosa 2020
archival pigment print; A/P
107.3 × 193.5 cm
Collection of the artist
Commissioned by Juddy Roller
Photographer: Rone

SELECT REFERENCE WORKS

GEELONG GALLERY COLLECTION

Florence Royce
Eucalypt flower vase c. 1935
hand-painted and gilded porcelain
Geelong Gallery
Gift of Florence Royce's
students, 1939
Photographer: Andrew Curtis

Florence Royce
Large bowl c. 1930s
hand-painted porcelain
with gilt edging
Geelong Gallery
Bequest of Dorothy McAllister, 1987
Photographer: Andrew Curtis

Florence Royce
Fruit dish 1930–50
hand-painted porcelain
with gilt edging
Geelong Gallery
Bequest of Dorothy McAllister, 1987
Photographer: Andrew Curtis

Florence Royce
Cup and saucer 1930–50
hand-painted porcelain
with gilt edging
Geelong Gallery
Bequest of Dorothy McAllister, 1987
Photographer: Andrew Curtis

Marshall Claxton
Portrait of Mrs Hugh Chambers and her daughter Hester 1853
oil on canvas
Geelong Gallery
Gift of EV Gayer, 1965
Photographer: Andrew Curtis

Robert Dowling
Mrs Margaret McArthur of Meningoort 1856–57
oil on canvas
Geelong Gallery
Purchased with the generous assistance of the Trustees of the Howard Hitchcock Bequest, and with additional support from the Friends of the Geelong Gallery, 2001
Photographer: Terence Bogue

Julian Ashton
Portrait of Louis Buvelot 1880
oil on canvas
Geelong Gallery
Purchased 1949
Photographer: George Stawicki

Tom Roberts
Portrait of James Quinn 1912
oil on composition board
Geelong Gallery
Purchased 1948
Photographer: George Stawicki

Frederick McCubbin
A bush burial 1890
oil on canvas
Geelong Gallery
Purchased by public
subscription, 1900
Photographer: Andrew Curtis

Oswald Rose Campbell
The finding of Buckley 1869
watercolour
Geelong Gallery
Gift of Robert Short, 1937
Photographer: George Stawicki

Hans Heysen
Gum trees in Flinders Ranges 1936
watercolour over pencil
Geelong Gallery
Gift of Mr and Mrs Brian Baulch
and family in memory of Mr and
Mrs SS Baulch through the Australian
Government's Cultural Gifts Program, 2011
Photographer: George Stawicki

Alexander Webb
On the You Yangs 1870–89
watercolour and ink
Geelong Gallery
Purchased 1995

George Lambert
The black hat 1920s
oil on canvas
Geelong Gallery
Purchased 1930
Photographer: George Stawicki

Esther Paterson
Portrait of Betty Paterson 1939
oil on canvas
Geelong Gallery
HP Douglass Bequest Fund, 1939
Photographer: George Stawicki

Ernest Buckmaster
Self portrait 1940
oil on canvas
Geelong Gallery
Purchased 1941
Photographer: George Stawicki

William Dargie
Portrait of the artist's wife 1940
oil on canvas
Geelong Gallery
JH McPhillimy prize, 1940
© Roger Dargie
Photographer: George Stawicki

ARTIST ACKNOWLEDGEMENTS

Rone would like to acknowledge and pay his respect to the traditional Owners and Elders, past, present and emerging of the Wadawurrung People of the Kulin Nation, on whose lands this exhibition is presented.

Rone thanks the Geelong Gallery, and the many generous funding partners that have supported the delivery of the exhibition and its associated publication, programs and promotion (as detailed elsewhere in this publication).

Special acknowledgement to the curator of this exhibition Senior Curator, Lisa Sullivan; Exhibitions Manager, Pip Minney; Deputy Director—Development and Commercial Operations, Penny Whitehead; Retail Manager, Jade Kellet; Building and Spaces Coordinator, John Stabb; Registrar & Collection Manager, Veronica Filmer; Elishia Furet, Learn & Audience Engagement Manager; administrative staff; volunteers; and Jason Smith, Director & CEO. It is only with the Geelong Gallery team's trust and passion that this 'less traditional' exhibition could be possible. Thank you.

Tyrone would also like to thank his incredible support network: exhibition team; family; friends; lenders; and collectors. Specific thanks goes to Alice Goulter for support; Sandra Powell and Andrew King for consultation; Hannah Marshall for administration; Carly Spooner of Establishment Studios for set dressing; Mo Wyse for production; Nick Batterham for music; Callum Preston for set building; Will Harvey and Lloyd Knowles for art assistance and installation; Ed Fraser and David Hooke for build assistance and installation; John McKissock for lighting; Chris Matthews of Defero Productions for filming; Tony Mott for behind the scenes photography; Peter Hatzipavlis for photographic post production and printing; Chris Dewhurst of Lite M Up for photographic lighting; Teresa Oman for modelling; Warwick Fabrics; GH Commercial; The Rangis for additional help; and Edward Cramer and Kyle Reeve of Tope Lane for our offsite build location. All without which this exhibition would not exist. Endless gratitude to you all.